C000215786

Better
Bed Manners

Better
Bed Manners

Anne Balliol &
Ralph Y. Hopton

BODLEIAN
LIBRARY
PUBLISHING

First published in 1936 by The Citadel Press, London
This edition published in 2023 by the Bodleian Library
Broad Street, Oxford OX1 3BG

www.bodleianshop.co.uk

ISBN 978 1 85124 619 9

This book was first published in the 1930s.
It reflects the views and attitudes of the period.

Cover design by Dot Little at the Bodleian Library
Designed and typeset by Lucy Morton of illuminati in 10 on 14 Scala
Printed and bound in China by C&C Offset Printing Co., Ltd
on 120 gsm Chinese Baijin pure woodfree paper

British Library Catalogue in Publishing Data
A CIP record of this publication is available from the British Library

Contents

'Even the kindest people are savage at night.'
—*Sir Walter Scott*

Bediquette

A BRANCH OF EDUCATION

IN AN EARLIER TREATISE we took the great public upstairs and showed them the most universal thing in their lives, which is bed. We gave them a few elementary ideas on how to get into it, how to lie in it correctly, and how to get out of it.

The darlings have shown violent interest in these instructions.

They have been taught for years how to eat asparagus and green peas, and how to write a formal letter to the Archbishop of Canterbury. They know what to wear when invited to a society wedding. Such things are merely etiquette. Hundreds of teachers have written about them, all ending at bedtime.

Our book goes higher. It goes straight into the bedroom. It discusses bediquette, the new social science intended for people so clever that they do not just hang up their good manners every night with their clothes.

This is the first complete book on how to be knightly, nightly. We commend this subject to every intelligent reader as an important new branch of public beducation.

In Bed with a
Teacher of Manners

THE GREAT TEACHER'S dinner party was coming to an end. Without bustle or confusion, each guest was saying goodnight and thank you to the hostess.

Deft servants helped the ladies to adjust their wraps, and the gentlemen to find their hats and coats in the cloakroom.

What a well-managed party it had been! How delicious the sherry with the soup, the white wine with the fish, the red wine with the joint! How beautifully the napkins had been folded, each containing a dinner roll. How correctly the knives had been laid at the right-hand side of each plate!

Yes, it had been a lovely party. Not a flaw in it anywhere. As each guest said 'goodnight and thank you' in well-modulated tones, the great teacher of etiquette made some graceful, correct little remark like: '*Dear* Mrs Dusenpeffer, so *good* of you to come.' All the men wore white ties and waistcoats with their tailcoats. All the ladies were perfectly dressed for the evening—none more perfectly than the great teacher herself.

In her restrained yet expressive voice, when the last guest had gone, she said: 'Good night, Bung,' to the butler. And then, because it is a mark of breeding to be appreciative of good service, she added: 'Everything was very well done, indeed.'

'Good night, madam,' replied the excellently trained butler, with a slight bow. It would not have been correct for him to thank his mistress for a compliment. All that remained for him to do was to put out the two cats, Etty and Quetty, and then retire for the night to his own butler's pantry, where convention required him to guard the silver.

The great teacher walked gracefully upstairs.

No human eye was on her, but a true lady never slouches. Mentally she reviewed her party. She had seen the way the Archbishop ate asparagus.

She scratched him off her mental list for her next dinner. And that flighty Mrs Constant Wreeder. She had hurried into the dining room without waiting for Mr Crumpelwaite to offer his arm.

The great teacher sighed. Well, her own manners had been above criticism—surely an inspiration for every guest. She shut the door of her bedroom. And with it she shut every thought of good manners out of her mind.

Instead of getting undressed, she just came to pieces.

Her underclothes lay in a puddle on the floor.

She put her hair into curlers and smeared her face with cold cream.

She looked at her husband, who was happily reading himself to sleep, and said, 'Well, Harry, is your firm going into bankruptcy or not?'

Then she asked him to get up and shut the window.

Then she turned on the wireless.

Then she turned it off, and brought the conversation back to her husband's financial affairs.

Midway in this disagreeable chat she saw a fly

on the ceiling. In a sudden effort to kill it, she trod heavily on poor Harry's solar plexus.

A bit later she was sound asleep on her back, snoring loudly.

In the morning she jumped up, dragging the bedclothes off Harry. Without bothering to tuck him up, or even to notice if she had wakened him, she breezed over to her desk. A happy thought had struck her.

'Well-bred people,' she wrote, 'demonstrate the exquisite courtesy of good manners at every moment in their lives.'

How to Go to Bed

THIS CHAPTER is for the conjugal couple alone.
Others may skip. We are not suggesting that
you will skip for joy because you are not one
half of a conjugal couple. If you are alone,
however, and go to bed with no human eye
upon you except that of a dormitory master, a
house mistress or some such person, you can
dispense with ordinary politeness. Just fall into
bed the best way you can.

But are you a wife? Then you have been ex-
asperated all day by house-to-house salesmen,
and by tradespeople. Your bridge game may not
have been prosperous. Your motor-car drive may
have been harassed by reckless policemen. When
your husband came home, you may have had to
break the news to him that he was expected to
take your mother and yourself to dinner and an

evening of chamber music at the Whiffenpoofs—whom he abhors.

You have come at last to the final stages of mutual exasperation. You are the martyr of the party, but your husband looks as if he were standing heroically at the stake. Very well. Here is your chance to give him a real surprise.

The surprise will come when he drives the car into the garage. Instead of leaping out and finding your way at once with the electric torch to your back door, you can stand patiently while he shuts the garage doors. There is always one door that works rather easily, and you can even help with that. Then light him past the coil of wire in the path, through the scattered ash bins and across the croquet lawn, if you have one. A great man, recently dead, once said there is nothing worse to walk through, after dark, than a croquet lawn—except a graveyard. So even if your mother is impatient to get in out of the damp, try to prevent your husband from sprawling over the hoops, and from falling upstairs on the kitchen steps.

In that strange, boyish, impractical head of

his, he always dimly expected these little attentions on the part of his squaw.

When you are safely in the kitchen, it is time for a stupefying remark. Here is a good one, warranted to delight the surliest male. Say: 'Wouldn't you like a whisky-and-soda before going to bed?'

At this point, your mother will be so appalled that she will hurry upstairs, leaving her son-in-law to his horrid orgy. Surely, the glass of sherry served by the Whiffenpoofs before dinner should be enough for any man who wants to keep his head clear for next day.

But it isn't enough. After a moment of surprise, your husband will look at you and say: 'Why, yes—I really hadn't thought of it, but I would like a drop of whisky very much indeed.'

9

All this time, you have stood convincingly by the sideboard, with the sort of expression which Circe donned when receiving her well-known visitors. Of course, you are not really going to turn your husband into a swine. If he is a tee-totaller, you can easily substitute his usual total of tea. Otherwise, take out of the refrigerator a bottle of soda water, extract some ice cubes from their chilly little coffin, place them in a bowl, arrange some cigarettes, biscuits and cheese on a tray, and have everything ready when your husband wanders back with the whisky bottle. He will then sit down and enjoy himself. If the cat happens to be mewing around, and looks prepared to put up a stiff argument before he is thrust outdoors, do the thrusting yourself while your husband quaffs.

Then is time for stupefying remark number two. Say: 'Make yourself comfortable—I'll see that everything is shut up for the night.'

While this remark is producing its effect, you can nimbly return all the supplies to their place and put the bottle back in its cupboard. As soon as you have entered your bedroom, assure yourself that your husband's bed (if a twin) is turned down, and that his nightclothes and slippers are neatly laid out on it. Then slip into your best-looking nightie or pyjamas, leave the bathroom in that almost surgically spick-and-span condition which men demand at their clubs, and await the reaction.

This reaction may not be immediate. It takes some time for any idea to penetrate any masculine intelligence. But sooner or later, a husband treated by his wife as he would expect to be treated by even the least capable house man will say: 'I have managed to keep about two hundred pounds away from the creditors—and you not only want a new evening gown but we both need a little cruise to Bermuda or somewhere.'

All of which is a proof that men are not so unobservant and indifferent as they seem. The very same man who drove home in a cloud of sullen boredom, wondering aloud why people are willing to annoy themselves with fussy food and meaningless music, may under these deft manipulations prove as charming a room-mate to you as he was to the boys at school. One whisky-and-soda on retiring—or any other potation, from brandy to buttermilk—makes the average man forget the dullest dinner and sends him to bed in a glow of goodwill.

He will be still more amiable if, when he starts to brush his teeth, he does not find your gloves soaking in the washbasin and looking like a nest of very cold pickled eels.

Now, are you a husband? Have you learned to retire without preliminary discord? What are perfect going-to-bed manners for you?

This problem is not so simple as it seems. Your technique is something like that we have outlined for your wife, but it must be far more subtle. Otherwise she will think you are just playing a part.

Do not overact. It may produce sudden domestic harmony, after years of connubial squalls, if you merely start wearing clean pyjamas every night. You might even, very cautiously, take a bath before turning in. The spectacle of a thoroughly clean man, dressed in spotless clothes, is just as pleasing to a normal female at bedtime as it is at lunch—or any other time. The man who comes lurching up to bed from the billiard-room, with chalk on his face and cigar ashes in his finger-nails, will be all the better for a good wash. And if his evening has been a long one, he will be all the better for a shave. We claim that many a man would catch the 8.05 a.m. train comfortably, instead of catching the 8.25 by the skin of his teeth, if he would shave at night instead of in the morning.

This is a terrific reform, far too radical for the ordinary man. Shaving in the morning is a ritual. It doesn't matter if the water is cold, if the only new packet of blades has been lost, if the hand is unsteady after too few hours of sleep—the average businessman has it deeply ingrained in his sense of propriety that he *must* shave before he goes to the office. At night he could do a leisurely, even artistic, job. But no. He is determined to present a freshly shaved face to the people on the platform, to the ticket collector, to the crowd on the Underground, and to the office boy who is distributing his letters.

The fact that he presented his stubbly jowls to

his wife, at bedtime, is of no importance to him. That is what wives are for.

It will please your wife, however, if you can manage to get to bed without encrusting her toilet soap and hair brushes with cigarette ashes. It will also please her if some night you can forget to wonder audibly why a woman wants a filthy cat around the house. It will enravish her if you make even a feeble effort, off your own bat, to fix the window blind which has been balky for a year.

But again—don't overact! Do these things naturally. Let them happen the way a glacier moves. Slowly, slowly! If you reform completely some night, it will sow the seeds of enduring suspicion. Your wife thinks of you exactly as modern hospital attendants think of their mental patients. Never will she believe that you have all your buttons. You are to be condoned, if not applauded, for undressing by gravity. (This consists in unfastening your lower garments at the waist, and letting them all sink on to the floor. If you are *very* neat, you probably then give them a place-kick on to a chair.) Your wife picks up after you more than you think, and smiles without rancour as she picks your pipe out of the butter-dish, when you have sprinted out of the door to catch that 8.25 train.

So it will never, never do to remodel your bed manners overnight. Your wife's idea of a really attractive man is that Woofwoofski fellow, who played the violin at the concert. He spent all the afternoon, probably, having his nails polished—while you, in the seven minutes you had to dress after coming home, couldn't even find your nail file. Never mind. Your wife was there in the pinch with an orange stick. She understands more than you think about the heroic, almost uncomplaining, rush in which your days are spent. Don't compete with the fiddler-man. Let him have the field to himself.

But this advice doesn't mean that you can relapse entirely into grateful barbarism. You are probably snorting with indignation at the idea that it might pay to hang up your clothes neatly, and even to take a bath, and even to shave. As for fixing the window blind, what do we think you are? A mechanic? No. We doubt if you are mechanical enough to do it, sir. We have often failed ourselves.

But we have suggested some ideas which can charm and even enslave the most unreasonable of women. If your night life at present is a sort of war of attrition, with both sides grimly holding on to their positions, you may accomplish much with a few strokes of strategy. In time of war, why not prepare for peace?

Going to Bed Under Difficulties

We have discussed going to bed under calm and normal circumstances—just the ordinary quiet family evening. But suppose the conditions aren't quite normal. What then?

For one thing, no two people ever agree about bedtime. Children will argue with you interminably that it is much too early for them to go to bed. Adults are a bit less quarrelsome—at least, outwardly. The strongest-minded ones always win. After all, form is form, whether you are talking about lawn tennis or bedtime.

The only man who ever laid down a plausible rule for knowing when it is bedtime was George Moore, the great Irish writer. He said that a man should get a good skinful of champagne, go to bed when he's sleepy and get up when he's rested. Such a rule is too Utopian for this mad machine age. The champagne part is the catch. If you expect to earn the champagne, you will have to get up long before you're rested. If other people give you the champagne, they will keep you up long after you're sleepy, dancing with the least attractive members of their parties.

So we present this rule merely as the bright but impractical dream of a fiction writer—something you may hope to do 'when your ship comes home'. The only ships that have recently come in are receiverships, and you surely aren't looking forward to one of them. But if you do have a pleasant evening, and come home with the conviction that you have had enough champagne for once, all the rules we have laid down are off.

Never mind an additional 'nightcap' before you go to bed.

Never mind the cat. Just avoid stepping on same. It will get underfoot in the most incredible way. Dodge it, jump over it, circumnavigate it somehow.

Never mind shaving. Never mind neat disposal of your clothing. With your mind set on other things, you will probably put a boot tree into your silk hat, and hang your trousers on the towel-rack—if you try to be neat about such details. Never mind taking a bath. Your whole object is to get to bed as quickly and quietly as you can.

In our other book we warned you that the recumbent and apparently slumberous figure of your wife is not really slumberous at all. She has been lying awake worrying because you did not appear, and now she is worrying about you because you did. No snatch of any song sung at the banquet will appeal to her. If you *must* talk, get it all out of your system on the way home—address it to the back of the taxi driver. He will pretend not to hear you, too.

But he won't be there in the morning to tell you, with alarming detail, just what you said.

This is all we have to say about this particular difficulty in going to bed—don't hum, don't sing, and above all, don't talk.

But there are other kinds of difficulties.

How shall you behave, in order to seem both mannerly and charming, if you and your wife have been so delightfully entertained in town that you have missed the last train to East Suburbia Gardens, or wherever you live.

You can't register at a good hotel in evening clothes and without luggage.

Old-fashioned people had this delusion so strongly that they used to sit up wretchedly all night in the railway station, waiting for the 6.33 train in the morning. Timid couples still do.

But there is a worn, domestic look about every husband and wife, when inspected together, which registers instantly on the night-clerks at any hotel that deserves to be called good. Go to the hotel without shame. You will be instantly shown to a room, and perhaps given a nice little emergency bag containing plenty of comforts for the night.

In the morning you can rakishly array yourself in your evening clothes, adjust your hat at a jaunty angle, button your overcoat up to your neck, telephone the office that you're 'calling on the trade', and go home for daytime clothes and a spot of sleep.

Don't write to us if this plan fails because your wife is so darned pretty that the night-clerk just didn't believe you. You are merely the exception that proves our rule. Be satisfied that you chose your wife so well, and take her to a supper club for the rest of the night.

Now for other difficulties in going to bed.

There will be a fine one when you and your wife, and those nice Joneses, and poor little Miss Follansbee, are all obliged to lodge for the night in some farmhouse that has just one spare bed for the five of you. This may follow a motoring mishap in some remote corner of the woods. Or maybe you got off the well-posted trail on your hiking trip. Or maybe your private aeroplane ran out of gas over one of the less-populated counties.

No matter how it happened. What to do?

Under rigid old-fashioned etiquette, you and

Bill Jones would have sat up miserably all night in the kitchen, while the three ladies shared the bed. Now, you all five share it—laughingly, and without a speck of false shame. Just spread your blankets or overcoats on top of the bed, and sleep on top of them, all five of you.

Avoid any reference about being as snug as a bug in a rug. You may be *exactly* as snug. If so, pretend not to notice.

This five-in-a-bed convention will give you and Bill Jones a bit of rest. Far more than you would get in the kitchen chairs. As for poor little Miss Follansbee, this will prove the most exciting and ribald adventure of her life. She will tell about it to her dying day, and always with shrieks of laughter.

The Seven Great Problems of Marriage

Hurrah! You are in bed. The day is over. The Wiffenpoofs' dinner is over too, and you have many hours of blissful slumber ahead of you.

You have paid heed to the suggestions in the earlier chapter. Your night clothes are becoming. Your face (if feminine) is not dankly glittering with perfumed mutton tallow (cold cream). You are a highly civilized couple, in bed at last after a toilsome day. Hurrah!

Hold that cheer. It would be a grand thing if you could now yield to that enchanted unconsciousness which all the poets recommend. 'O magic Sleep!' wrote Keats; and again: 'O soft embalmer of the still midnight, shutting, with careful fingers and benign, our gloom-pleased eyes!' John Milton had already written of 'the dewy-feathered sleep' and Shakespeare of 'the honey-heavy dew of slumber'.

But this honey-heavy dew will not come regularly to you until you have faced Seven Great Problems, at least two of which have so far defied all human ingenuity. Science has no solution for them. Perhaps if you can suggest a universal remedy, your name will go on history's roll of honour with Edison and Pasteur.

Here are the problems.

I. IN WHAT SORT OF BED WILL YOU SLEEP?

It has been settled that most people like the comradeship of sharing a room. It is far from settled that they like the comradeship of sharing a bed.

Crowned heads of old solved this problem nicely. Either they snuggled together into a state bed about as big as a small battleship, or else they flouted comradeship by having separate apartments on different floors of their various palaces. Even so, it is said that 'uneasy lies the head that wears a crown'. And you will hardly be able to try the separate apartments idea. Your home may not be a palace. You may be a bit cramped for separate apartments so long as your mother-in-law, your Aunt Mary, and her three lively children are making such a nice, long, indefinite visit to you.

So, for your cosy conjugal bedroom you will have to choose between twin beds or a double bed. Women are said to prefer the double bed, on the ground that they are more afraid of the dark than men, and 'naturally prefer the comforting proximity of a bedfellow'.

We are here quoting a high authority. He goes on to say that women know that twin beds cost twice as much to buy as double beds, and also twice as much in bedclothes and laundry. Or darned near it. Twin beds also take up one and a half times as much space as double beds. In spite of these objections, they are selling much, much faster than double beds.

It seems, then, that the average husband is not 'comforting' as a bedfellow. His 'proximity' is very likely an affair of loud snores, of throwing his arms and legs about as he sleeps, and of grabbing the blankets off his spouse and winding them round himself like a cocoon.

We shall discuss the cures for these disorders in their proper place. Meanwhile, there is just one safe rule in buying a double bed. Buy it *big*. The biggest we have found on the London market is sixty-three by seventy-six inches, which is no real Jumbo of a bed, but is still far better than the ordinary ' double', in which you feel as if you were in a couple of bus seats, if not in a bureau drawer.

The biggest bed ever made was 'The Great Bed of Ware'. This comfortable object is almost eleven feet square, and is reverently preserved in a museum. It made such a deserved hit with Shakespeare and Ben Jonson that both mention it in their plays. The last time it was used, a century or two ago, it is recorded that 'five tradesmen frolick'd in it with their wives'.

Even if you could get along without the other four tradesmen and their wives, something like the Great Bed of Ware should be in every home that spurns twin beds.

Recent improvements in double beds include

making one half of them firm for the Spartan lady, and the other half soft for her pampered consort (or the other way round, if you are that kind of people). But see page thirty-seven for a still more-needed improvement.

2. THE PROBLEM OF LIGHT

Is your room-mate or bed-mate a reader? Then he or she will want to pursue this hobby in bed. Only three years ago we thought this problem was insoluble by science. And lo! science has realized that the one who is trying to sleep is insufferably annoyed by the wide-spreading light of the bedfellow who loves to read. You can now buy what we called upon scientists to produce—a sort of electric spotlight that projects a beam of light directly on the book, and nowhere else.

Humanity has been fairly bellowing for such a gadget. If inventors had hurried up with it, instead of frittering away their time on things people didn't know they wanted—the telephone, for instance, or the self-starter for motor-cars— innumerable divorces might have been saved.

The problem of morning light is more difficult. You can shut it nicely out, as your ancestors did, by sleeping with the windows shut and the blinds  tightly drawn. If, on the other hand, you love fresh air so much that you sleep on the upstairs verandah, you can buy a sort of burglar's mask that will exclude the light—and that may even exclude a burglar, by making him think that a fellow craftsman got up there before he did.

3. THE PROBLEM OF VENTILATION

Although this goes hand in hand with the problem of light, as suggested in the previous paragraph, it really requires a bit of independent research and mutual flattery before you can settle it. It is a strange fact in all railway travelling, and in the operation of buses, stores, theatres, etc., that a person who loathes fresh air always prevails over a person who likes it.

You are sitting in a stuffy, overheated railway carriage. Finally you lose your temper and open a window. Instantly your neighbour slams it down. If you venture to disagree, he calls the guard to enforce his wishes. Guards are always on the side of the majority; and the majority is terribly afraid of coolness, and even more afraid of draughts.

Before marriage, therefore, it is a useful thing to know if your intended feels about fresh air as you do. Argument won't help. Everybody has an unconscious memory of those centuries when it was universally thought that 'the night air is poisonous'. Our grandsires nailed their windows shut every autumn, and stuffed cotton wool into cracks in the window frames. Draughts were considered deadlier than daggers.

Air-conditioning is coming about slowly, because many people feel that it somehow *does* let a lot of air into the room. Were it called 'air-omissioning', it would have swept the country. One of its most attractive features, to many people, lies in the little sign which reads 'This carriage is ventilated —please do not attempt to open the window.' As if most people would!

If you have broken the human race's inherited dread of fresh air, be sure to marry somebody who thinks as you do. Otherwise, until air-conditioning arrives everywhere—and enables you to do surreptitious things with a little valve after your consort is asleep—you will disagree every night. To you, the breeze from the open window seems assurance of health and repose. To your bedfellow, it is merely a proof that you want to bring the rigours of the Arctic into the room.

4. THE UNSOLVED
PROBLEM OF NOISE

Mayors proclaim against noise. There are dreadful penalties in London and other cities for tooting your horn after bedtime. Motor lorries backfire. Firemen love to zoom through the streets with their sirens shrieking. The roar and clatter of the traffic is London's familiar lullaby.

We know a noise more destructive to connubial felicity than any of these things.

It is the common snore.

This is the first of the two great nocturnal problems that haven't yielded to science, although science—having invested years of time on such baubles as the alternating current—is now taking up shoring in a serious way.

It seems to be definitely proved that only contented people snore. Their facial muscles relax, their mouths open. The mouth must be wide open before snoring can be done loudly and efficiently. So one remedy is to make your bedfellow a bit less contented with his or her lot. If recent business conditions, starting about 1929, haven't done this, the chances are that nothing can do it.

The next remedy is a chin strap. This is on the market, and it does keep the mouth closed. Unfortunately, no snorer is ever absolutely persuaded that he or she is guilty. It is far easier to assume that one is being traduced, maligned and insulted. So in presenting a chin strap to your bedfellow, if you have enough courage to do it, you might suggest that it is an adjunct to beauty—a preserver of the contours of the throat and jaw, a preventive of double chin.

Unhappily, any person vain enough to fall for this good selling point in favour of the chin strap will be quite vain enough to study its appearance in the mirror. This appearance is not good. Even the handsomest horse loses grace and charm when his nosebag is adjusted, and the result of wearing a chin strap is much the same.

So the last resort (after a trifling operation for adenoids has been tried) is to plug up your own ears. Oddly, most people fail hopelessly at this. They use absorbent cotton wool, which is a good conductor of sound. It may keep water out of your ears when you are swimming, but it won't keep snoring out. Rubber is also no sound-proofer. What is on the market now, in the form of ear-plugs, are little gadgets made of wax and cotton, which are but partially effective.

Something better is now being designed, and when it comes out our faith in science will be restored considerably. Even so, trying to plug your own ears is a palliative—but not a cure. If the snorer is contented enough to sleep through a fire alarm, and if you are sound-proofed enough to sleep through it too—why, you might both be burned in your bed. Or to think of something less disagreeable, you might miss a midnight telephone call from a lawyer in Australia, who is trying to tell you that you have inherited a fortune.

Alas! The snoring problem still laughs at surgery, science and sleepers.

5. THE PROBLEM OF PILLOWS

This is, comparatively, a trifle. Men like their pillows harder and more numerous than women do. Lie right down on the pillow counter in the shop, if need be, and make sure. Get your bedfellow to lie down in turn. You may give the gentlemanly shopwalker a few hearty laughs. But there will be no crowd to see your little test; we never saw a crowd at a pillow counter, unless unwanted goods were being marked down.

Your head is going to be on a pillow for a third of your remaining lifetime. Why not test the pillow almost as carefully as you would test a pair of shoes, or anything else which you buy? Pillows do come in various shapes, sizes and degrees of softness. You *can* get what you like.

6. THE PROBLEM OF WAKING UP

This is vexatious. It springs from the fact that we all sleep with varying intensities. Some do their heaviest sleeping early, some late.

King George V is said to have solved the little problem of royal punctuality by keeping all the palace clocks half an hour fast. You can possibly do this, and fool yourself enough to catch the 8.05 at least one day a week. But you can't fool any bedfellow in the world into waking up naturally just when you do. And you can't find an alarm clock that will wake a heavy sleeper without also arousing a light one.

So you will just have to reconcile yourself to a little unpleasantness every morning, and smooth it over all you can with fair words.

7. THE PROBLEM OF WARMTH

This is the terrible problem, the enigma from which our baffled scientists reel away in despair.

Given two people in two different rooms, there is no problem. One can shiver under six blankets and two eiderdowns. The other, on the same night, will be gasping for air under nothing but a sheet. Each is happy after his or her own fashion.

Put those people into twin beds, and the problem is still not unconquerable. The shivery one can wear bed-socks, and use a hot-water bottle, and wear flannel pyjamas, and have as many blankets, etc., as he pleases. The warm-blooded one can go the limit in stripping the bed and herself (or himself, as the case may be).

But now put these people into a double bed.

Absolutely *no* blankets have ever been made that will stay over one sleeper, and not over the other. Diagonal folds are of no use. Half-sized blankets slip off you. Finally you have to compromise the whole matter. The shivery bedfellow pulls a lot of bedclothes over both the parties. The warm-blooded one presently kicks them off again.

This is exactly the sort of thing that makes war between nations. It makes the Thirty Years War look like a weekend when it starts in a married couple's life.

We have no remedy.

There is one thing that helps the shivery combatant a great deal, and that is a realization that a whole lot of warmth went out of the world with the old-fashioned feather bed. When you slept on one of those, you were warm. In fact, you soon came very nearly to a boil. That is because feathers are a fine insulator. You'd be a goose if you swam in the Arctic Ocean. But a goose does, if you see what we mean.

Unhappily, cold-blooded people have given up feather beds, and now sleep on mattresses full of spiral springs. Each of those spirals delivers a fine, cool current of air just where it can hurt you most.

There is no insulation whatever in a modern mattress. It keeps you just as cold as if you were sleeping on the floor. Colder. It *pumps* the chilly air against you, as you stir in your sleep. Piling bedclothes on top of you is no good. Well, it is some good. But not enough.

The remedy is a thin woollen blanket under the bottom sheet. This will warm you surprisingly. It will also warm your hot-blooded partner, perhaps even to boiling point.

But, as we said, science hasn't solved the problem of how two people can gratify their own individual ideas of necessary warmth in a double bed.

The largest manufacturer of beds in this country says gloomily that he doesn't think science ever will. But we think that the double bed of the future—when Utopia comes—will be marked H on one side and C on the other, like your bath taps. How the Utopians will achieve this we don't know. They will do it somehow— perhaps on the very day they learn how to abolish war, to extract gold from sea water, and to cure a common cold.

The Seven Pillars of Desertion and Divorce

1. An all-night mosquito hunt, in which you step several times on your sleeping partner's abdomen.
2. Any nocturnal conversation concerning lack of money in your family.
3. Permanently cold feet.
4. Cold cream and curling pins.
5. Pyjama pants that don't match the jacket.
6. Any dentifrice flavoured with wintergreen.
7. The lack of any dentifrice at all.

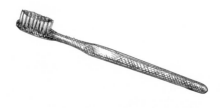

How to Get Up

WITH THE KEENEST ANTICIPATIONS we attended a recent performance of *Romeo and Juliet*, with a great actress and a great actor in the title roles.

Here is the great, classic bedroom scene in all literature. May we refresh your memory with a few of its magical lines:

ACT III, SCENE V
The Same. Juliet's Chamber
Jul. Wilt thou be gone? It is not yet near day.
It was the nightingale, and not the lark,
That pierc'd the fearful hollow of thine ear...
Rom. It was the lark, the herald of the morn...
I must be gone and live, or stay and die...
Enter Nurse
Nurse. Madam!
Jul. Nurse!

Nurse. The day is broke. Be wary. Look about.

(*Exit Nurse*)

Jul. Then, window, let day in, and let life out.

Rom. Farewell, farewell! One kiss and I'll
    descend.

Somewhere in this conversation (we were too much interested in looking at the handsome bed to notice just where) Romeo *does* get up. What a surprise! Was he tousled, rumpled, blear-eyed, and in terrible need of a shave?

What a question! It shows how little you know your Shakespeare, who is the imaginative and romantic wizard of all time.

This is what happened. The great actor sprang athletically out of bed. Not a hair was disarranged on his handsome head. His cheeks glowed with the healthy pinkness of grease-paint. He was fully and even richly dressed in a complete suit of clothes. Complete? Why, he even had his shoes on. He could have strolled into his office and been the best-groomed man there, without so much as pausing to comb his hair in the washroom.

A bit later Juliet also rolled nimbly out of bed to receive an early morning call from her mother. Juliet, too, was absolutely ready for the day. Through our strongest opera glasses, from our seat in the front row, we couldn't see a thing to criticize in the neatness of her hair, her clothes and her complexion. And the bed itself, though it had been slept in all night, was just as smooth and unruffled as if it had been on exhibition in some 'model room' in one of the great departmental stores.

What do you say to that?

We say it is a lesson to us all. We say it is no wonder that Shakespeare has made such a success. Not only were Romeo and Juliet able to bear each other's scrutiny at daybreak, and be the very best dressed young couple in Verona—they were also able to look their very best to all the 1,780 people in the theatre, which was sold out for this occasion.

Such is the magic of a great dramatist, and a great pair of actors. We envy them. We envy the actor even more than the actress, because a comely young lady somehow does manage to be more presentable in the early mornings than even the best-dressed young man.

We have been present at the risings of too many young chaps not to know that they are frightfully rumpled, bristly, yawning, dishevelled and horrid-looking birds whenever you wake them up—and all the more so if the time is about six o'clock in the morning.

So this is our best advice. Take a leaf from Shakespeare's book, and go to bed with all your clothes on, correctly dressed for the coming day. Lie so absolutely still that you don't muss up the bed. Get up nimbly, with lines of deathless poetry on your lips. Then you will charm 1,780 people, if by any chance they are present to see you, and as for charming your bedfellow, well, you know the effect that Romeo produced on Juliet. And you will catch an early train, and gain great favour at the office; all by being really prepared for the day, and by showing—as this Romeo did—such absolutely perfect morning manners.

But perhaps you *can't* do this. Perhaps a single trial will convince you that the heyday of romance has gone. Perhaps you will mess up your clothes dreadfully if you sleep in them. Then we have a word of advice for you, young man.

Spring out of bed every morning like a lark springing out of its nest, and run, do not walk to the bathroom. Close its door behind you and don't emerge until you are bathed, shaved, brushed, manicured and otherwise prepared for inspection.

Ladies will do well to accept the same good advice.

In Bed with a Nice Person

PERHAPS this experience is still ahead of you.

Without this book to put you on guard, you would have some very rude shocks.

You surely have memories of sleeping in youth with a large, soft teddy bear. Or was it a doll? Or a kitten? You naturally expect your human sleeping partner will be as soft as the teddy bear, as quiet as the doll, as gentle as the kitten.

The surprise that will come to you may be the most terrible in your life.

Not one of your expectations will come true.

So perhaps it is just as well if you happen to be a friendly, old-fashioned, matey kind of person from a large family where flocks of guests were always being invited to spend the night. You were always being doubled up with a sister or brother. Or one of the little guests was shoved right into bed with you. Then you know what to expect. Human anatomy is no surprise to you.

It is to the absolute beginner in sleeping double that this chapter is addressed. Your first shock will come from the discovery that even the nicest person—even a plump, handsome, really beautiful person, once voted by his friends the handsomest man at Oxford—is actually a skeleton most insufficiently padded at the forehead, chin, shoulders, elbows, hips and knees.

And if your prospective bedfellow is a lady— yes, even a lady who has put on five pounds since she won a beauty contest at Folkestone in 1933—why, even this buxom bedmate is also a skeleton with no padding whatever at the points we have mentioned above.

Such grievous wounds can be inflicted by the bony forehead, the sharp chin, and the hard shoulders, elbows, hips and knees that their use is strictly illegal in the prize-ring.

Watch One-Round McCafferty hit Sailor Glutz with his elbow when he thinks the referee isn't looking. Hear the storm of hisses from even the bloodthirstiest fans in the gallery. Watch the

Sailor try to get a bit of his own back, by butting McCafferty in the face. What yells of 'Foul!' and 'Throw the big bounder out!'

But the two foul fighters in the ring are paid to take punishment. You are not. You are just trying to get some sleep.

Crash! comes your bedfellow's elbow into the tender place just below your ribs. Or smack! comes his knee into the small of your back. He doesn't mean anything by it. He is just 'turning over in his sleep'.

This is the moment to toss him out of bed and then have a short, intimate chat with him on the subject of lying quiet.

But suppose he is a nice person, and was bed broken long ago as the result of living in a large family with too few beds for all the people who used his home as a free lodging house.

He is quite likely to tell you that the female skeleton is just like the masculine one—only a bit sharper at the corners, and at the ends of the fingers. He may say gently that he wishes you would keep your claw out of his eye. You didn't mean to put it there. You just thrust out your arm as a defence mechanism against a mosquito. (You can almost hear the mosquito give a low, hoarse chuckle of satisfaction as your husband rubs his eye.)

We seem to be bearing down hard on this skeleton matter. That's because it is so unexpected to all beginners in bedmanship. Although they have taken their own skeletons to bed with them every night of their lives, it is a merciful provision of nature that you *can't* stick your elbow in your own eye, or deal yourself the so-called 'kidney punch' with your own knee.

The very nicest people, by the way, often have a 'skeleton in the cupboard'. That's the nicest place for it. Hang it up there and it may rest peacefully for years. But if you must have it on you at all times, then learn to control it.

Don't pitch and toss in bed like a ship at sea. As the poet so nearly said:

> *Rest—and your wife rests with you,*
> *Thrash—and you sleep alone!*

The more nearly you achieve the modern fashionable figure, the more you look like an umbrella in its case, the more deadly weapons you really take to bed with you. Remember that an umbrella would lie still. Try to do this. You won't succeed. Photographs taken at short intervals during the night reveal to science that nobody really does 'sleep like a log'. People are always squirming, and writhing, and rolling over in their sleep—they assume all the strange poses of Robert Benchley in the movie. Then they snap out of these comical poses with a flurry of nature's weapons that would make Joe Louis jump out of the ring.

Bedfellows soon get tired of being butted, gouged, slugged and otherwise maimed. They put their heads together (without enough of a bump to produce two fractured skulls) and work out a rough set of Queensberry Rules for their own protection. What are some of the other great surprises in your beducation?

Perhaps you have married an 'encroacher'. He is the sort who unconsciously shoves you, inch by inch and foot by foot, across the bed. He doesn't know he is giving an imitation of a star player in a rugby scrum. He is sound asleep.

You become aware of him, dimly, when you feel his jaw against your neck, or his clenched fist in the region of your spine.

You groan, and move away. Instantly he occupies the captured territory. In military language, he consolidates his position. Perhaps he gains another four inches by breathing heavily on the back of your neck. You move. He leaps into the place you have just occupied.

Very soon you are on the absolute edge of the bed. You are teetering on it, ready to plunge. Now you have what is called 'the falling dream'. You think you are plunging down, down into space. And you *will* plunge, if your funny old encroacher has his way with you.

Long-suffering people at this point try to foil the encroacher by climbing over him. This feels a good deal like changing places in a Canadian canoe. But you manage it. You have a faint hope that the encroacher will keep on travelling in his original direction, with the happy result that he will crash to the floor himself. You hope he will.

Vain hope! He will come right back after you, now prodding, now pushing, until he has driven you across the centre-line of the field (pardon us, the bed). Now you are on your five-yard line, now on your goal-line, and there is nobody present to shout 'Hold 'em!'

What to do. A lot of wives want to solve this problem by using a revolver or a heavy sash-weight. Even if they had to stand trial as the result, they say it would be far less of a trial than what they have gone through.

We have called such a bedfellow 'the encroacher'. In the courts they have a legal name for him. They call him 'the respondent'. They try to make him pay high for this form of extreme mental (and sentimental) cruelty. For that is the worst of it. He really does it because he feels drawn to you, darn him.

THE HUMAN CATERPILLAR

Another sort of bedfellow is really a caterpillar in disguise. In his sleep he grabs all the bedclothes and winds them round himself like a cocoon, leaving you bare.

You wake, chilled to the bone. You find this

great human caterpillar snoring away beside you. You unwind him. With chattering teeth you remake the bed. You fall into stupor, only to find that he has done it all over again.

What a pity that, if you left him to himself, he would not emerge from his cocoon as a beautiful butterfly. But he won't. No wings will ever sprout on him. In the morning, when you are sneezing and shivering in the first stages of pneumonia, he will wake up smilingly and say:

'Where *did* you get that snuffle, Gwendolen? I slept as warm as toast all night.'

READERS-,
TALKERS- & EATERS-IN-BED

These are minor afflictions. You can bilk a reader out of his or her secret joy in your sufferings by installing the spotlight mentioned on a previous page. Of course, he or she just can't be allowed to read a newspaper that rattles in your ears like musketry. A book is better. Also duller—so it will put the reader to sleep much faster.

Choose bedside books for their soporific

qualities. Follow the advice of the stupidest assistant in the worst bookshop in town. Avoid all the good detective stories. Tell the library man you want volumes of serious importance. Poetry is a real lullaby to most people, and a 'stream of consciousness' novel is nearly as good a sleep-producer as the trickle of a real stream outside your window.

As for the talker-in-bed, never argue with her. That only wakes her up, brushes the cobwebs out of her eyes. She may say the most bitter things about your earning capacity, about your relatives, about the bad habits the children have inherited from you. Agree with them all. Agree with grunts and other sounds indicating that you are very, very sleepy. Turn the conversation into a monologue. Most monologues you ever heard put you to sleep, didn't they?

In the morning, refrain from asking whether the little monologuist beside you is talking still or again.

Just spring nimbly up, with no questions at all.

Now for the eater-in-bed. A lot of women regard breakfast in bed as the one supreme

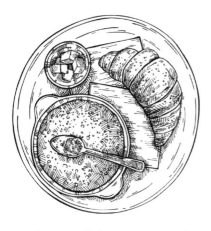

luxury of their lives. During the honeymoon period (the twenty-four to seventy-two hours which follow one's wedding) she may invite you to share this meal. Suggest two trays and two tables, one on each side of the bed. A deluge of hot coffee is painful, and bad for the sheets. So is a fumbled egg, while a muffed muffin will deposit crumbs where they can irritate you most.

As for the miscreant who keeps stuff on the bedside table to nibble or munch at night, hanging is too good for him. Fill the stomach with food in the evening, and you will get through to breakfast all right. Try to peel an orange, on your back, and it will squirt accurately into your bedfellow's eye. Try to eat a biscuit without showering crumbs into the bed. The sharp deposit of grit from this source will make any night sleepless.

These are the common types of bad bed-fellows. Avoid them or reform them. There is no middle ground.

'But,' you say, 'I have read this chapter under false pretences. It was headed "In Bed with a Nice Person," but it describes only the worst kind of pests.'

True. And yet you have forgotten somebody. How about yourself? Aren't you exactly the sort of nice person with whom anybody of cultivation would be charmed to—

How to Invite Somebody to Bed

You 'date yourself' far more by what you say than by the way you look. The use of worn-out language (especially slanguage) is fatal to the best efforts of your barber and tailor, your gymnasium instructor, and all the others who try to make you seem youthful and sprightly. And if you're a lady—why, you may spend your allowance ten times over at the dressmaker's and the beauty parlour, and still be recognized for a grandmother if you use a grandmother's wisecracks.

If you say: 'Let us retire!' you date from the 1870s. If you say: 'Let's hit the hay!' you date from the 1880s. If you speak of your bed as 'the feathers', you are using slang of nearly as ancient vintage. To speak of going to bed as 'flopping' is also not very new. In fact there is nothing safer and more modern to say than 'Let's go to bed.'

But people do get tired of saying this over and over again, especially if they have to say it several times every evening, before good results are attained. Comical bishops in novels usually vary it by making up a phrase such as 'Let's all go to Bedfordshire!' But this also is old.

To be thought young and dashing you need a wholly new piece of slang. It is always piquant to make it up yourself, and not depend on seeing it in the newspaper, or overhearing it at a party. Here is the way to proceed.

It was funny to call a bed 'the hay' for a few years after the mattress *was* stuffed with hay. But your mattress is now stuffed with selected horsehair, full of correctly tempered hour-glass springs, and magically insulated with fleecy felt. If you don't believe us, cut it open. Or read the advertisement of that mattress.

You would surprise and perhaps charm almost anybody, even your husband, if instead of saying 'Let's hit the hay!' you said: 'Let's hit the selected horsehair, full of correctly tempered hour-glass springs, etc., etc.' But maybe this is too long to learn by heart—and it certainly won't sound funny twice.

What you need, to refresh your way of speaking, are some good, reliable words that mean 'bed'. A short list includes bunk, berth, pallet, crib, cot, shakedown, *lit* (French) and *palang* (Hindu). Then you want a few good words that mean 'lie down', 'yawn', 'snore', 'take a rest', and so forth. You might trust the dictionary, but never trust a dictionary too far. Or you will find yourself saying to some startled person, who never went to a classical school, something that he or she won't understand.

Only if your wife went to Somerville can you say: 'I am somniferous. Are you statuvolvent? Shall we oscitate in our palang?'

It is really simpler to say: 'Let's go to bed.'

Bed Manners
in a Haunted House

Nobody believes in ghosts—in the daytime.

You don't have to visit Glamis Castle, or any other house that is reputed to be haunted, to feel the thrill of a supernatural experience.

Any house at all will do. Merely be alone in it all night.

Let's assume, for instance, that you have just inherited your great-uncle's fine old stone villa near Windsor or Bath, or some other historic town. Your husband was going to be with you for the first night in it, but is delayed by business.

Instead of being chicken-hearted, and taking a room at the hotel, you decide to spend the night alone in the house. The sunset looks lovely over the rose garden. You are glad you are so far from all neighbours. Here is peace and repose at last.

So you think.

You light the lamps. How cosy it is not to have electricity. The lamps make spots of light in the dark, high-ceilinged sitting room. You try to read. A thought strikes you. In *which* of the bedrooms did your great-uncle's father kill himself?

You are almost sure it was in the big south bedroom, where you have made up a bed for yourself. How ridiculous to worry about a thing like that. However, you go upstairs with a lamp, and make up your bed in the south-east room, instead.

What a dark, gloomy-looking room it is—and how the floorboards creak. You are glad to get into bed. You are glad you have a good book.

Somehow, the book fails to grip you as it should.

What a strange lot of noises you hear. In town you have the rumble of civilization all around you. Trolleybuses, motor cars, lifts, people walking in the street. But town houses don't seem to squeak and clatter and groan at night.

You blow out the lamp. Heavens! Where did you put the matches? In a panic you fumble all over the room for them. At last you find a paper match-folder in your handbag. You light the lamp again. Your fingers are shaking. You lie for a long time wishing the lamp would make the room *really* light. It doesn't. It just brings out those awful black shadows in the corners.

Now you hear somebody coming upstairs.

You break out into a cold perspiration. But nobody does come—it was just the floorboards creaking. After a while you blow out the lamp again. You must really get some sleep.

What is that strange noise in the attic? Somebody is walking there? Or is it just imagination? Actually, a lot of rats live in the attic—and what they can do, scurrying back and forth at night, would chill the stoutest heart. You tell yourself it is only rats. Your husband and you will find a way to exterminate them soon.

It is terribly hot and airless with your head under the bedclothes but you can't help it. When you stick your nose out for a breath of air at last, you see something that absolutely chills your blood. You are looking at a ghost.

It is a long, long time before you realize that the ghost is nothing but your own clothes across the back of a chair, lit up by a ray of moonlight through the window.

Meanwhile, you have been lying on your back with chattering teeth, and your heart pounding. You are afraid to look, and afraid *not* to look. And when you finally persuade yourself that your great-uncle's father's ghost has not visited you, as yet, you hear something scratching at the window on the other side of the room.

This is just a branch of ivy, stirring in the rising wind that precedes a good brisk thunderstorm. You tell yourself that it's nothing but the ivy. Scratch! Scrr-rr-atch! It sets your teeth chattering again. And you are always afraid of thunderstorms. You wish you dared to get up and shut the window. You wish—

Flash! Boompety-boom-Boom! What a storm it is! You never heard a worse one. Cr-rr-ack. Whang! Boom! You know it will knock the rickety old house down, and bury you in the ruins. Swish—hrrmph—Bang! What was that? Something enormous and scratchy seems to be sliding down across the window. The window panes break with a clatter of glass. By now you have probably fainted, and are lying in a puddle of cold rain from the broken window. You won't know till the morning that it was nothing but a branch ripped from the elm tree that smashed your window.

And even if you escape this shock, you will be waked at intervals from your uneasy naps, through the night, by the series of horrible noises that only an old house can make. Somebody is always stalking upstairs. Somebody is always prowling around over your head. That blood-curdling 'whoo-whoo-whoo-oo-oo' in the garden doesn't frighten you after the first five minutes. It is not your great-uncle; it is only an owl. But interior sounds in an ancient house have never been fully explained. Perhaps they are only the woodwork cooling off after the heat of the day. Perhaps they are caused by rats and squirrels in the walls. Perhaps—and who doubts it after just one night spent listening to them?—they are made by ghosts after all.

In the morning your husband will come bounding in. He will be hearty and smiling. Although you have been scared out of ten years of your lifetime, you will greet him with a brave smile.

'Last night on the train I envied you,' he will say. 'How lovely and peaceful it is in this dear old house!'

The next night, and for the rest of your existence in the old homestead, it is good bed manners to share a room and a bed. Console yourself with the thought, well known to every society for psychic research, that no two people have ever seen a ghost at the same time. You have to be alone to get the full effect.

Suzygophobia

THIS IS THE OLDEST DISEASE in the world, though it has never had a name till now. You know it. You probably have it. Don't tell us you don't know what it is. You've heard of Claustrophobia, and Hydrophobia, and even Silurophobia, haven't you? Silurophobia means 'car fear'. We have coined Suzygophobia from the Greek word *suzygos*, which means 'yoke-fellow' or 'mate'.

Do you have Mate Fear?

Do you have it worst at night?

Do you approach the conjugal bedroom fearing everything that may happen to you in it? Would you rather plunge into a jungle that may contain a tiger than plunge into a bed that surely does contain your mate?

The cure for this awful disease is to leave this book where your ferocious mate will find and read it. Enclose it with a bunch of Gloire de Dijon roses, or fold it into a bath towel, as your means may permit.

If the book doesn't teach your mate the rudiments of good and gentle behaviour, your last recourse is a club. (The Union Club and the Carlton are considered to be perhaps among the most refined, exclusive and desirable hideouts in London.)

The Freedom of the Seas

PATRIOTIC PEOPLE are always talking about this. England fought for the freedom of the seas in 1812, and fought Germany for it in 1917. We are always ready to fight for it. What is it? Why do people adore it so?

You can't find out from reading any book, even this one. You will just have to go on a good, long cruise. Across the Atlantic to Albany isn't long enough, and it's only the freedom of the Hudson River. What you need, to find out about the freedom of the seas, is a cruise to the North Cape, or round South America, or round the world.

On such a cruise, people behave with far more freedom than they ever do at home.

There is no limit. Of course, you have heard talk about 'the twelve-mile limit'. That was plenty of margin. Even if you are on a boat as big as the *Normandie* or *Queen Mary*, it is still only a fifth of a mile long. You can behave with sixty times more freedom than that.

Back at home, in East Sheen, Brighton or the Channel Islands, or wherever else you may reside, you aren't used to having people crash into your bedroom at any hour. And probably your bedroom isn't in direct telephonic communication with a bar. But now you can order drinks as soon as the steamer leaves the pier—now you can have anything your guests want served to them at any minute.

The serving is done by your steward. This word comes from the word 'stye-ward', meaning, in ancient days, the man who took care of the pigs in their stye.

Whenever you aren't having a small, informal cocktail party in your stye—excuse us, we mean your cabin—you will be enjoying a large, informal one in the saloon. (This word comes from the word saloon, a drinking bar; originally a public room used for a specified purpose in an hotel or place of public resort.) As a change from the large party you can go and have a small one in the cabin of any fellow-passenger at any time, day or night.

One hundred and fifty-eight days of this will bring you back to the dock, and probably to the doctor, via Havana, the Panama Canal Zone, Honolulu, Singapore, Angkor Wat, Liverpool, Cherbourg, Port Said and Marseilles. We haven't named these ports in proper order, but you won't have been in proper order when you saw them.

The ideal itinerary for a long cruise (we throw out this suggestion gratis to the steamship companies) would be as follows:

Rye Beach.
The Bar (or entry to a harbour).
Rhum (island in the West of Scotland).

Bed manners on such a cruise are, naturally, a matter of always being prepared for anything. You are generally just taking a short nap between the McWhooshlebain's late party last night and the Burdock-Jones' early party before luncheon today. With old-fashioned courtesy, Mr Swatch—that funny fat man from Friskney—taps on your door before entering. He is followed by the steward, bringing your morning bracer. In such a case, a lady always wants her *robe de nuit* to be very fresh and becoming, and her cabin to be as free as possible from the cigar ends, decaying *hors d'œuvres*, half-empty bottles, melting bits of ice, and other souvenirs of Archie McWhooshlebain's visit a few hours before.

As Swatch bursts in, with a merry shout of 'Hit the deck!' or 'Show a leg!' or 'The sun's over the yardarm!' your bed manners are on test as they can't possibly be at home.

Receive him with easy good manners. Ignore the mess in your room. His own room is much worse. Don't feign heavy sleep. If you do, Horatio Swatch (who is absolutely intoxicated by the freedom of the seas and by other things) will woo you from slumber with a hearty pinch. And if you do not feign sleep, he will probably woo you anyway.

This happens every morning, all round the world. If Swatch is absent any day, his place will more than be filled by somebody whose whole previous experience of travel has been in hotels, on cheap day excursions and on the tripper steamers at the seaside. Such a gentleman saves up for years and years to take a cruise. And when he takes it—

Well, these few hints will give an idea what the freedom of the seas actually is, and why all patriotic people are ready to fight for it to the last drop of their blood.

P.S.—If you see a great, grey war vessel dashing through the water on some errand of destruction, don't be frightened. It is just a bottleship, too.

How to Be a Charming
Convalescent at Home

This can't be done. But you may have to attempt it, none the less.

Perhaps you have known what it is to be handsomely overpaid for anything you happen to call your work. Whenever you felt a twinge in your throat or tummy, you could hurry off to a specialist. He bundled you into a hospital. That was that.

The 'profit system' in America didn't last long. It turned into the 'prophet system' during which all the nation's leaders prophesied that prosperity was 'just around the corner'. They might as well have told people it was 'just around the cornea'—meaning it was all my eye!

Then came the 'proffy system' directed by professors or 'profs' who never earned large salaries anyway, and didn't see why anybody needed more than a few dimes in their pants. Under such a system, you would have surely decided to avoid much indulgence in specialists and hospitals.

You have made up your mind bravely to endure your next illness in your little white bed at home.

Your ancestors were born, slept, lived much of their lives and finally died economically in their own beds. Why can't you?

You can! In fact, you must. So here is a brief and, we hope, not too terrifying outline of your next disease.

THE ONSET OF YOUR ILLNESS

The disease will start just before your evening meal. You will discover: (1) that the great tobacco companies can't make a cigarette fit to smoke and (2) that your wife never has any decent drinkable stuff in the house. You feel like a hero as you bravely swallow the nauseating mess she shakes up for you.

At dinner you remark that a pig couldn't eat such a mess. You scold the innocent children for such trifles as screaming and upsetting their soup. You go early to bed with only a few earnest criticisms of your wife for not having the missing top button sewed on your pyjamas, and for allowing the children to make such a noise over their homework.

When you do get to sleep, your savage mood is neatly reflected in a series of frightful nightmares.

So frightful are these dreams, indeed, that we cannot possibly analyse them for you. First you dream you are trudging barefoot over an ice floe. You feel yourself falling down a crevasse. Then the chilly crevasse turns into a lake of boiling oil in which you explode with a loud 'pop'. A little later, packs of wild cats pursue you through tropical forests, and finally you fall into a quicksand full of rattlesnakes and scorpions.

Your dreams are something like that—but much more vivid, of course.

Dawn comes at last, and never was it more of a relief. You have wound the bedclothes into a sort of huge coil on one side of the bed. The arm and leg under that coil are dripping with perspiration. The other arm and leg are freezing cold.

Your wife straightens out this mess, and says she hoped you slept well. She heard you muttering to yourself. She proffers you an aspirin, saying it is a good thing to take to head off the 'flu.

The 'flu, indeed! You have had one shattering glimpse of your tongue in the bathroom mirror. Your head is splitting. Your eyes are bloodshot. You are in the grip of something that is obviously more deadly than any mere 'flu.

What time is it? It is past eight o'clock and you have now missed all your trains—your regular train and the later one which you regularly catch. All right. You will go right back to bed. Perhaps a day's complete rest will fix you up.

PROGRESS OF A DISEASE— THE FIRST DAY

The maid now enters with a breakfast tray. Bridget has always been too modest to invade your bedroom. Now she gives one frightened glance at the tousle-haired, unshaved, wild-eyed and cursing wretch in the bed, and beats a hasty retreat. You turn away with a groan from the well-laden tray which your wife balances beside you on the bed.

We may remark here that it is the height of bad bed manners to forget the tray and fall into it while you are throwing yourself about. You look bad enough already. If you smear your pyjamas with marmalade or poached egg, if you make a huge dark stain of coffee on the sheets, you will only add to your misery. But after your dreadful night you are now too weak to throw yourself about. You don't fall into the breakfast tray. After the food on it grows stone-cold, your wife sighs and lugs it away. She goes to the telephone.

'Dr Rooby,' she says, 'I wonder if you can conveniently come and look at my husband today. He had rather an uncomfortable night... yes... yes, there is so much of this 'flu about.'

Hoarsely, you bark: 'But I don't want a doctor. We can't afford a doctor. We owe all the money we'll ever see to doctors already.'

This is a brave remark though an untruthful one. You do want a doctor. You want the best doctor in the world, and you want him in five seconds. You try to take stock of your symptoms. Your headache is worse, but you now have a sore throat to match—and this would take your mind off your head if a still more enormous agony were not surging from your chest down to your stomach, and up again.

With all this, you have a burning fever. You are scared. You could bear these various pains if they weren't so frightening. You are a strong man. But this is no time for you to die. And your wife has asked the old country practitioner to call at his 'convenience'. His convenience, indeed. Well, he may crawl around in time to write out your death certificate...

You are dying. You know it. Your wife returns to find you breathing hoarsely, with your eyes fixed in a glassy way on the ceiling.

'Dr Rooby says you must certainly stay in bed today,' she remarks. 'There is so much of this 'flu about.'

Then she calls up her sister, and arranges for the children to go there after school and stay in her house. This call makes all your symptoms immensely worse. Her call to the doctor confirmed your knowledge that you are very ill, but this second call is the height of mental suggestion. Poor children—poor orphans! How will they ever grow up without their father's loving care?

Now your wife calls up your office, and tells the telephone operator that you won't be at business today. You are laid up with a heavy cold, and there is such a lot of 'flu about...

Even if everybody is determined that you have only 'flu—even if old Rooby has diagnosed you without taking the trouble to come and look at you—you know how quickly 'flu turns into pneu. Pneumonia. That hideous word burns in your brain. It burns for hours, while you wonder why old Rooby doesn't come.

A STRANGE FACT ABOUT DOCTORS

No matter how ill you feel, before the doctor comes, it is a strange and rather mortifying fact that you feel enormously better as soon as he enters the room.

Dr Rooby comes at last. You have braced yourself up. You tell him that he is looking fine.

You tell him that you are feeling fine. You ask about his golf. All the time he is sticking his icy little thermometer into your hot mouth, you are chatting bravely with him about little odds and ends of gossip. He tells you not to talk. He thumps your chest, feels your pulse, looks casually down your throat while you try to say 'Ah'. Then he goes downstairs with your wife.

Now it is a mystery of house construction that a poorly inhabitant can always hear every word spoken about him in his own house. Selectivity is perfect.

You hear Dr Rooby say: 'No, it isn't grippe. I'm not sure. I will arrange for a trained nurse at once. They are rather hard to get at the present time. I will be back in an hour. There is nothing to do at present but keep him very quiet, and, of course, let him avoid all worry.'

So you felt better while the doctor was in the room, did you?

How do you feel now?

The doctor confesses that he doesn't know what is the matter with you. Perhaps he *does* know and is merely sparing your wife's feelings.

Why couldn't he have put her out of the room and told you frankly—man to man—that you have one of the deadly diseases? Meningitis? Acute nephritis? Streptococcus? You groan and clench your hands.

Well, if this is the end, you can at least die game.

SETTING YOUR AFFAIRS IN ORDER

You wonder if you can stagger to the telephone. You decide that you can. Your bedroom slippers have been tidied up, and you have to walk bare-footed. This reminds you of your dream about the ice floe. You grasp the telephone shelf with one hand, and hold yourself up while you painfully call up your friend, Henry, the stockbroker.

'Henry, old man,' you croak. 'I am very ill. Listen carefully. I want you to get me entirely out of the market—sell everything. My will is in my strong box. I wish you'd go over to my office and clean out every drawer...'

Henry wants to know if you are drunk or dreaming, or both. Finally you convince him you

79

are serious. He promises to do what you want. He says it is a bad time to sell. He listens with great interest while you tell him about a few private debts—large ones—which you instruct him to pay at once.

You hear your wife coming up from the kitchen. She is horrified to find you shivering, in your bare feet, at the 'phone.

You manage to make her understand that you are setting your house in order, for her benefit. You totter back to bed. You know you are dying. Your telephone call has supplied any last bit of necessary mental suggestion.

Your fever mounts, and you sink into damp unconsciousness. You awake with the feeling that the hangman's hands are at your neck. It is only Dr Rooby. He has unbuttoned your pyjamas, admitting a blast of icy air, and he is staring at your chest.

'Doctor,' you whisper. 'You must tell me what the matter is. I can bear the truth. Do you know what disease I have?'

'German measles,' says the doctor, 'and a light case at that.'

PROGRESS OF A DISEASE— CONVALESCENCE

Those blessed words of Dr Rooby's ring in your ears. Now you know what it is to come back from the jaws of death. Hurray! You sit up in bed. Your temperature may be 102 degrees—but what's that? You may be peppered all over with red spots—but what are they? You want a drink, and a lot of the breakfast you spurned at eight o'clock, and the morning paper, and maybe a small steak.

Meningitis—pooh! Pneumonia—pfft! You grab a cigarette. Never in all your life has one tasted so good.

Dr Rooby advises you to stay in bed, to avoid using your eyes too much, and to live largely on liquid food. You suggest to him that whisky is a food. He shakes his head.

Your wife's expression has changed. She clearly realizes that for the next week she will have to wait hand and foot on a fully grown man with a nursery disease. Just as this glad thought comes to her, Bridget taps on the door and admits a formidable old woman with a suitcase.

'The trained nurse,' announces Bridget.

Dr Rooby takes the nurse away in his car. This is a break. With so much real disease around—like the 'flu—young and pretty nurses have been all snapped up. Besides, there's nothing the matter with you. You absorb a large bowl of soup, a dozen biscuits and a couple of doughnuts. Hurrah for the chance to lie lazily in bed, reading a thrilling new novel in print so large it doesn't hurt your poor, bloodshot eyes.

You read the thrilling new novel till a terrible thought strikes you. Henry! What did you tell *him*? What intimate facts did you give him about yourself? You bound out of bed. Your bare feet don't flinch from the cold floorboards. You admit to the startled and cynical Henry that you were a bit crazy, earlier in the day. Has he sold you out of the market at a staggering loss? Has he sent enormous cheques to your creditors? Has he been snooping around your desk?

Whether Henry has done all these things, or only a few of them, there is nothing to do now but to go to bed and get well. This takes a good deal of patience. By the end of the second day you are wondering why there is no decent reading matter in the house. You can't decide whether to reread *Ivanhoe* or *Goodwin's Greek Grammar*. You are frightfully tired of the little red spots which looked so absolutely welcome only yesterday.

Your office calls up to know whether there is anything much the matter with you. They want you back. The Bjornsen deal is evidently on their minds.

Wearily you review the Bjornsen deal. As nearly as you can remember, Mr Bjornsen is hostile to your senior partner, Mr McGlook, because Mr McGlook got much too chummy with Mr Bjornsen's wife on that North Cape Cruise in 1929. But Mr Bjornsen came down from the university in 1895, and you took your degree at the same university in 1921, so that ought to make a bond between you. You are supposed to go to the Bjornsen office, and introduce yourself first to Hoopenberg, whom you never met as an undergraduate, and through *him* you are to meet Mr Bjornsen, and...

Well, it's something like that. How your head aches! You are supposed to know—no, you are supposed *not* to know—about the unfortunate scenes on the SS *East St Louis* away back in twenty-nine. Hoopenberg will never suspect at this late date that it was your blackball which kept him out of the club.

How your head aches!

That's the worst of trying to read in bed all day, it makes your head ache. If you were only at a hospital, you would have some visitors. But nobody calls on a man who has measles at home.

You discover, meanwhile, that your home is a veritable throbbing hive of human activity, all day long. In the morning you hear the endless *Whoo-hoo-hoo-oo* of the electric vacuum cleaner. Why can't Bridget use a brush, and some elbow grease, and help cut down your electric bills? Thank the Lord the doorbell operates on a battery. It rings all the time. There are hundreds of callers and Bridget holds long converse with each one. You thump for her.

You have, by this time, stopped answering the telephone yourself, although it offers you many extraordinary opportunities to buy furniture, hardware, groceries, insurance, stocks and shares, annuities and other things. And you find the wireless bringing you its messages more furiously, even, than it does in the evening.

Your wife remains calm, goes to her favourite place for morning coffee and her various afternoon clubs and bridge classes. The third day of your illness ends.

It brings you an afternoon call from Traskberry, the only man who had the prudence to sell out in twenty-nine. He isn't afraid of your measles. No, bless him, he would probably call on you if you had the bubonic plague. He has nothing to do but cut his lawn, and transplant his begonias back to where they were yesterday, and take his dogs for a walk. A poorly acquaintance is a godsend to him.

You aren't fond of him, but you have him brought straight upstairs. You wring his hand. Once you thought him a bore, but now you are delighted to listen to his gossip, and to play piquet with him. He smuggles you a drink. It tastes like nectar. Good old Traskberry.

Next morning you kill a lot of time shaving and doing your nails with your wife's manicure tools. You feel quite well enough to go back to work. Maybe the Bjornsen deal has been settled.

You ring up your secretary. It hasn't. Mr McGlook calls up later. He wants to know how you really feel. When will the doctor let you out? You say the date is still indefinite. Yes, you have every comfort. Yes, the doctor is first class. Yes—or no, rather—you *didn't* know that old Mr Bjornsen's married daughter is a member of your wife's Culture Circle. Yes, that is an angle which might well prove valuable.

Confound it! To what a pass has business fallen when your boss expects to sell five hundred thousand gross of beard combs to a deadly enemy because his daughter is in your wife's Culture Circle. You ask your wife about this. No, that awful little Mrs Gunderstein did not get as far as that—she attended as a guest, but the members failed to elect her. No, your wife hasn't kept up the acquaintance.

You look very neat and tidy by now. There is a nice colour in your cheeks, because you are sleeping so well and getting such a luxurious rest. Two days pass. Traskberry comes every afternoon. You really think you might stay at home for a whole week.

His last visit is expected on Friday afternoon. You really might have gone to town that day. But you would merely have got involved in that hopeless Bjornsen deal. Far better to stay home one more day. Mr McGlook has called up your wife, and she has told him that you are still very far from well.

She does not tell him—and why should she?— that tomorrow you and she are going to motor down into Sussex, to stay with those nice Faxons.

Soon after lunch you hear a masculine tread downstairs.

'Hullo, you old rascal,' you call, in clear, bell-like tones. 'Come on up. I'm just putting on my golf shoes, and I'll either play you eighteen holes, or we'll go for a good long walk with your wolf hounds. Come right up.'

But it is not Traskberry who comes up. It is Mr McGlook, who has come to see with his own eyes just what is the matter with you.

Don't try to be nonchalant at this point. It is far better to admit that even your wife's friendship with Mrs Gunderstein is not enough to put the Bjornsen deal through.

A Woman's Best Friend is Her Hot-Water Bottle

One bedfellow that never loses its charm for any woman is her hot-water bottle.

Inventors have burst upon the modern scenes with electric warming pads, and with gadgets which you can plunge into hot water and which are guaranteed to stay hot for hours. We are not talking of these things.

We are talking of the common or chemists'-shop hot-water bottle, invented in 1873 by a man named Reuben Fuzzletisch. You can buy it anywhere. It may be still the 1873 model. It may grow old and decrepit in your service. Its screw top may be leaky. It may look as if it were going to burst at any minute. No matter. The woman who has become dependent on it will cherish it to the end.

All through that last dismal, sleepy rubber of bridge at the Spoopendykes' house, with the cold draught simply roaring across the floor and chilling her feet, her eye will brighten when she thinks of the faithful hot-water bottle hanging on its bathroom hook at home. Though she is far too tired to join you in the midnight snack recommended on an earlier page of this book, she is not too tired to get the bottle and light the heater, or put the kettle on the stove. Filling her nocturnal hot-water bottle is a rite that outlasts her prayers, her faith in the League of Nations, and all her other most cherished little credos.

Watch her as she puts the bottle into her bed and adjusts its genial, faintly gurgling shape to her chilly feet. Watch her as she shifts it to other suffering parts of her anatomy. You will wonder why men have erected statues to the man who invented nothing more ingratiating than the sewing machine. Why, if we hadn't told you the name of Mr Fuzzletisch you wouldn't have felt so strongly moved to subscribe for a statue to *him*.

If you are a man, and it falls to your lot to share a bed with a woman and a hot-water bottle, don't try to get it away from her. Any violent grabbing with your hands, or soccer football tactics with your feet, will burst it. This is one of the nastiest nocturnal adventures that can happen.

A MAN'S BEST FRIEND IS HIS DOG

But don't encourage your dog to think he's going to maintain his position on your bed after you marry. The snores, the scratching and shifting and also the aroma of your four-footed bedmate will be something to conceal from an innocent bride.

You may possibly solve this problem by inducing good Towser to go and get married himself.

Bed Manners in a Country House

Watch this carefully. It begins because you meet, at some party, a quiet little gentleman wearing eyeglasses and a pepper-and-salt suit. His name is something like Hart, and he looks very much out of things—embarrassed and shy.

You dimly remember that his family has for generations manufactured some staple article. Hart's Hartware, that's it. Ploughs. Barbed-wire fencing. Maybe teaspoons and war munitions. Or some stuff sold mostly to farmers. This must be a grandson of old Hart. Poor little fellow, he seems very shy. Somebody ought to have told him to wear evening clothes in a swell night club.

You take an interest in him. By the end of the evening, you and he and your wife are like kittens in a basket. Suddenly he asks if you wouldn't like some country air.

Why can't you run down to 'Heart's Ease', his place in the country? You'd get some shooting. Maybe your wife likes walking in the woods, or paddling a canoe on the river, and that sort of thing.

You get a picture, somehow, of a cosy, ramshackle old country house, where you can take supper in your shooting clothes, and nobody ever dresses up. You say you will be glad to come, if he cares to fix a date. You never expect to hear from him again. But you do.

He writes a few days later, fixing a date. You say to Susan that this proves it pays to be kind to outsiders at a party. Poor little Hart. It will brighten his dull days down there if you accept. And what a chance for a simple, sensible vacation, with no bothers! You couldn't think of Ostend or even Gleneagles, or Margate. Think of the clothes you'd have to buy. And the tips! And the hotel bills!

But this nice week at funny old 'Heart's Ease', with the wisteria over its door, and maybe a nice old couple making the porridge and mixing the drinks—why, even if you don't shoot as much as a rabbit, it will be splendid fun, and a *real* rest. Thank goodness Mr Hart got a night out, and that you met him and like him, the shy, unsophisticated little man.

You make no inquiries. You just oil up your gun, and haul your old shooting jacket and corduroys out of the trunk in the cellar. How good they smell! Now you know why a hunting dog barks for joy when he smells that good manly odour of gun grease, dried blood, perspiration, powder burns and so forth.

Your dinner jacket? No, indeed.

'But we may need evening clothes,' says Susan, doubtfully. 'Mr Hart may live very comfortably. Perhaps he'll have some neighbours in for dinner on Saturday night.'

You flout the idea. Belchertown is no winter resort. Mr Hart lives there to get away from London—he told you so, Evening dress would only remind him of the garish night clubs which he obviously detests.

You tell Susie that her five-year-old tweeds and a couple of sweaters, and those everlasting old brogues she brought back from London in twenty-eight are just what she needs. Not one penny need be spent in clothes buying. Hurrah!

Your train stops at Belchertown Junction at last.

For hours and hours it has been running through a bleak countryside of red clay and straggly trees, dotted with small, tumbledown cottages. Evening clothes? Absurd.

YOU GLIMPSE HEART'S EASE

Beside the station platform are a lot of rusty old flivvers and a cart drawn by a pair of quiet horses. You hope the cart is for you. It would be in the spirit of your simple, old-world trip.

But no. Farther down the platform is a yellow station waggon, glittering with varnish, and mounted on a Rolls-Royce chassis. The words 'Heart's Ease' are lettered on it in modest type, no more than eight inches high.

Oh, well—just one bit of extravagance on Mr Hart's part. It doesn't mean anything. Probably he snapped it up at a bargain during hard times.

'Isn't it wonderful,' you say to Susie, 'to be

travelling for once with just three bags, a gun case, and no trunks?'

Almost before you have finished this remark, one of the two liveried men in the station waggon comes forward.

'Mr Turtlebottom, sir?' he asks—and you have an uneasy feeling that he doesn't like your hat, suit or shoes.

You nod.

'If you will give me your tickets, sir, I will see to your trunks.'

'Oh, yes,' you say. Confound the fellow. He is intimidating you. 'Oh, yes, the trunks. I haven't seen the trunks. They are doubtless—er—on a later train.'

Now you are in the Rolls-Royce, gliding majestically through a tiny town. Speed improves when you reach the highway, but the drive takes an hour. You spend it trying to read one of the large labels which the man has affixed to your three old bags and gun case. You wish the leather of the gun case weren't cracking and coming off in large flakes.

You get tantalizing glimpses of the labels. The man's expression frightens you from trying to wrench a bag away from him. At last Susie sees what you see, and promptly demands her small bag. Your heads bend together over the label, which reads:

GUEST LUGGAGE
Heart's Ease House

Name of Guest—Mrs T. Turtlebottom.
Date of Arrival—January 7, 1936.
Date of Departure—January 13, 1936.
Via—Belchertown Junction.

Assigned to.	*Suite.*
Heart's Ease House.	....
Mon Plaisir.	....
Petit Trianon.	*Marie Antoinette*
Annexe No. 1.	....
Annexe No. 2.	....
The Village.	....

You look at this label and lick your dry lips. So there are six places to stay on the homestead, are there? How fast the car is going, and how much the road has improved. You are speeding through woods that look as if they'd been gone over with a vacuum cleaner. Every leaf clean and glossy, not a speck of underbrush. You see a herd of deer. Then a cock pheasant rises from the road, with a whirr of its expensive wings.

'How long before we get to the—er—estate?' you ask.

'We've been on the estate for the past 'alf-'our, sir,' answers the flunkey. 'You may now catch a glimpse of the main 'ouse.'

You do. It stuns you. Windsor Castle, but on a larger scale. Peacocks are strutting on its parterres. Now you have whizzed through the village, and past an artificial lake—a large one. Windsor Castle is out of sight now, but you are drawing up in front of a large building in the French style. You guess, correctly, that this is the Petit Trianon.

You are shown to the Marie Antoinette suite, a nest of silk hangings and gilt furniture.

Since you are too late for lunch at the main 'ouse, a pleasant little four-course *déjeuner* is to be served in your own dining-room.

Footmen are standing behind the chairs where you and Susie will sit. Alas, for your sensible, simple holiday!

NOW YOU CAN SEE YOUR BED

Your alarming valet has by now unpacked you. He has laid out your smelly shooting clothes, your torn sweater, and your woollen socks with large holes in their toes. And what has he laid them out on?

True to his traditions, he has laid them on a Bed—a Bed with a capital B.

It stands on a raised platform. It is a monstrous concoction of gold scrollwork, painted panels and heavy silk canopies. Instead of bedposts, it has figures of cupids embracing nymphs. It is so high that an ornate little gilt stepladder is provided to mount it.

You have looked at the panels. 'French, I suppose,' you say. You wife giggles hysterically. She says it is the real thing—an original French bed, no doubt used by Marie Antoinette herself.

The hussy!

'You and I will look lovely in that bed,' she snaps. You know that snap. It is a prelude to tears, to hysteria.

At this moment you must make a great decision. Either you and Susie can bluff things out, and try to find among the eighty-nine other guests dotted over many square miles of estate a couple of good Samaritans who will lend you the necessary wardrobes—or else, you can beat it at once.

Let's assume you have no friends whatever among the guests, that you are too proud to try to borrow a suit from Ponsonby, the valet (who is twice your size, anyway), and that you want to make a decent getaway.

IF YOU ARE POOR BUT PROUD

Summon Ponsonby. The varlet will come to you with a silly remark about being unable to find your evening clothes. 'White ties are being worn tonight,' he will say.

Pay no attention. Think of a town and think of a telephone number—no matter which and what.

If you can't think, Westminster is an impressive place, and Whitehall 1212 is a serviceable number.

Instruct Ponsonby to call that number, and to inform the First Secretary that Mr Thomas Turtlebottom will be with him tomorrow. That will take Ponsonby down a couple of pegs. Have him call up the garage for the station waggon, have him repack your rags, give him as little as your conscience permits, and ho! for the junction and any old train you can catch.

Susan will regret in afterlife that she never did sleep in that bed. But she can't have everything!

IF YOU ARE POOR BUT SHAMELESS

In any big house party you can always find *somebody* you know. It will probably prove to be those awful De Bracy Finkenvillers, whom you haven't spoken to at Scarsdale for ten years. You will now find them lolling in luxury. Go right up and fall on De Bracy's neck.

If you manage things well, you will emerge from this happy reunion with De Bracy's dinner jacket, with his second-best Burberry, half a dozen of his shirts, his spare pair of braces, and an absolutely foul assortment of his ill-chosen jewellery and ties. Thank Providence for this rich haul. If Susie has equal luck with Mrs Finkenvillers, you needn't 'phone that appointment till tomorrow.

You will have a night in Marie Antoinette's bed.

Do justice to the occasion. Conduct yourself with fitting gallantry. Brush up your French. When at three o'clock in the morning you come back, exhausted, from dinner and bridge and music and dancing in the main 'ouse, tell Susan what she wants to hear. Tell her that her eyes outshone all the candles in the great hall, or that Mrs Finkenvillers' horrid old dress didn't show any gap in the back.

Your French may not suffice for these elaborate compliments, but don't let that stop you. You know your Susan. Make a little ceremony of helping her up the gilt ladder. When you give your hand to steady her, say '*Enfin!*' (French for 'At last!') When she wants to

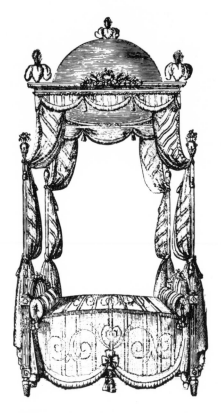

climb down in the morning, say '*Déjà?*' (French for 'So soon?')

Susan will give a little squall of surprise at finding the bed is made up with black silk sheets.

That is because Louis XVI was so tired of seeing women in white ones. Tell her this interesting historical fact. Be as much like an old-time courtier as you can. You may look anything but romantic when you take off De Bracy's black clothes and stand revealed in your old slumber suit—far too tight around the waist and too baggy in the seat.

But wear it with a flourish, as D'Artagnan would have done.

These chivalrous new manners of yours will remain a pleasant memory, when you recall your first (and last) visit to Heart's Ease. With slight logical revisions, they will also make a tremendous hit at home.

IF YOU AREN'T POOR AT ALL

There is an outside chance that you fooled little Mr Hart as badly as he did you. Maybe you are as rich as he is, every whit. Maybe you sized him up for a pleasant little plebeian, with no more millions than he has fingers and toes.

This is most unlikely. A multi-millionaire

can recognize another on sight, if not sooner. Their shabby clothes and shyness deceive all bourgeois people, but don't fool each other. Put two of them in any crowd, and they will soon be hobnobbing together. If one of them speaks to you, he will ask some unimportant question like 'How is your mother, nowadays?' But if he has anything important to ask, he will prowl around till he finds another millionaire and then he will say: 'Do you know what time it is?' or 'Have you got a match?' It seems as if he could accept important information, or any small favour, only from one of his own kind. Don't ask us why. Birds of a feather flock together. This applies only to multis—not to the common millionaires you meet everywhere, who dress as flamboyantly and talk as noisily as if they hadn't a bean.

Well, if you *are* a multi, and if you went down to see Hart, you wouldn't bother a minute with the Marie Antoinette bed. It would make you dizzy to lie in it. You would tell the houseman you can sleep only on an army cot. Or any old bedstead without box springs will do.

Would you bother about clothes? Not at all. Of

course, you could telephone to your town house to have a full wardrobe motored out to Gatwick Airport, and from there your private pilot could fly it down to you in time for dinner. But you'd just moon around the grounds all afternoon, being largely mistaken for a plumber or for the man who gives the baby pheasants their Mellen's Food.

Hart would find you at last—behind a toolshed—and the two of you would hold a nice long intimate conversation, leading up to the point that you will dine together in your shooting clothes, and that your favourite dinner is hamburger steak, pretzels and beer.

Then you can go to bed comfortably on the cot, and slide out early next morning for your own little place in the country.

So You Don't Sleep Well!

A really good sleeper does not have to woo the great god Morpheus. He goes to his nightly repose:

> *As one who wraps the drapery of his couch*
> *About him, and lies down to pleasant dreams.*

Take, for example, a lumberjack. The bunkhouse may be full of noise, lights, smells, smoke, and the shouts of his colleagues quarrelling over their cards. Do such trifles disturb him? Not a bit.

He strides to his bunk, pulls off his shirt, pants and shoes. Now he is under the blankets. His upturned face may be within two feet of a lamp, but in ten seconds you hear a *bzz-bzz-bzz* as rhythmic as a circular saw biting into a log.

Lots of city chaps are just as informal about falling asleep.

They may not actually *be* asleep when they come stumbling over their thresholds. Some instinct makes them hurl their evening clothes at a chair and kick off their pumps. Once in bed they are heavily asleep, just like the lumberjack. The great thing, obviously, is to be terribly tired, and to have nothing on your mind.

You can make sure of being tired by not going to bed at all for two or three nights.

So far this chapter is one long platitude. Not a bit of novelty in it. But now tiptoe with us to the bedroom of any person who sleeps badly.

Watch this person prepare for a night's repose. All through the evening, he told you he was a martyr to insomnia. Eyes gleaming dewily with self-pity, he assured you that he *never* gets a good night's rest. Every night is a sleepless night for him.

And why not? He sets up everything for it. Beside his bed is a large table, and on the table you notice a lamp, a water jug, a glass, a teaspoon, a packet of bromides, an assortment of other powders and pills, a plate of fruit, a box of cigarettes, a wireless, some cotton wool to put in his ears, a black bandage to tie over his eyes before sunrise, a bottle of whisky, a manicure set, a pack of cards, a thermometer, and a couple of detective stories.

Just about what a man would need to keep him amused and interested through an Arctic night.

But is our friend amused? Not he. He has been to the police station, and bought tickets for the Policemen's Ball, and asked the sergeant to enforce the ordinance against cars tooting their horns between midnight and eight a.m. The sergeant has told him there isn't any such regulation. There has been an argument—but no refund of the money for the tickets.

So our friend is a victim not only of insomnia but of police indifference to their duty. He wishes he could have his bedroom fully soundproofed. If very rich, he has done so. The effect is sepulchral. You feel that in this tomb-like room the wings of a single mosquito would thunder like an aeroplane motor.

But the 'victim' is gloomily hopeful that the soundproofing will exclude the chirps of early-morning sparrows, and the snorts of the milkman's horse. Let's leave him to his fun. The bedside table of his will keep him fully occupied all night.

Never a dull moment!

Not far out of London is a psychiatrist who has a short way with such sufferers. He gives them a few hours of carpentry, or work on a hand-loom, followed by about eighteen holes of golf, a dance at the country club, or a good stroll in the moonlight. Meanwhile they have had three square meals. The squarer the meal, the more circular the patient— but the doctor is right there to see that he gets his exercise.

Then he is shown to his room.

What?

No bedside table at all? No reading light? No orange or apple? Nothing but a bed, a bureau and a chair? And no way of getting out of that room until eight in the morning! Strong men turn pale at such hardships. Women weep with dismay.

They keep on pitying themselves for at least thirty seconds after their heads hit the pillow. Then—

Well, the good doctor has had to install a dressing gong that would resurrect many people out of any cemetery. His patients sometimes complain, whimsically, that they have nothing to do in their bleak little bedrooms but sleep.

This method, as you know, is called psychiatry. You can either pay several guineas a week for it, or try it without any expense at home.

Suppose you do try, and fail. Where are you going to get eighteen holes of golf in London? Are you going to tee your ball on the club doorstep, and see how many strokes it will take you to reach Wimbledon? You would be arrested. Where are you going to get a loom, and what would your boss say if you started to work it in the office? Good bed manners and good sense require, if you *do* have insomnia, to have it privately and not wake up the whole household. Worry and insufficient exercise cause it. The sharpest attacks come on the nights before you are going to fight some battle of Waterloo in the office, or when you just can't meet your overdraft at the bank.

You will wonder, after a few hours, why you ever were able to sleep. You will hear the traffic throbbing and roaring, as loudly as it ever does in daytime. To your aching ears it will sound louder. Your pillow will feel like a washboard. Your bedclothes will stick to you in clammy corrugations, No position is comfortable. All the rest of you aches, as well as your ears.

Steady now. If you go down and look for cigarettes, every floorboard will creak under your feet. You may trip over the cat. Yet you can't stay in bed. Yes, you can read a little—it will tire your eyes and make you sleep.

So you pick up the latest by Phillips Oppenheim. This author lives by making his customers gasp, by curdling their blood, by setting their hearts to pounding. When you get to the place where the international opium smugglers have Lady Geraldine Maltravers in their hellish power—and where only one man in Europe has the power to save her, and *he* is on his way in heavy irons to Devil's Island—why, when you get to that comparatively mild situation in the story, you will be beyond the aid of any sedative. But you probably will put the book down, and take a sedative. If it wouldn't wake the family, you would turn on the wireless. You do throttle it down and turn it on. Lively dance tunes. Lively police messages. You wish some intelligent announcer would say: 'You will now receive eight hours of silence.'

Nobody does. You turn off the entertainment. Phillips Oppenheim and the sedative are still struggling furiously inside you. You moodily go over, for the eighty-fifth time, the little speech you are going to make at the bank—or the little speech that you didn't make to Mr Higgenbottom at the office, when he said that your services were required no longer.

You're in for it. If you tiptoe to the sideboard for an orange, you'll wake up your mother. You're too tired to get up. Too tired to stay in bed.

Getting up is the lesser of these two evils—but you'll have to get up and get out, to work a real cure.

Don't put on a dressing gown and prowl around the house until everybody is awake and either cursing or consoling you after their fashion.

Get up, dress and go out.

There is one chance in a million, of course, that you will be robbed by a highwayman. But the fact is that you will seem to be a highwayman yourself. Innocent passers-by will shrink away from you as you swing along, with your hat down over your eyes.

What a busy place London is at night. Even the side streets. What lots of people are always up. What lots of all-night restaurants. After five miles or so, at a swinging clip, a hot dog tastes pretty good, a cup of coffee is nectar.

Gosh, you shouldn't have taken that coffee! It will only keep you awake. But you are interested in the pink dawn behind the tall buildings, now you're seeing it at your ease on a park bench, and not out of a taxicab window. It's exciting. If you weren't so terribly sleepy at this point...

If you weren't all tired out by hitting the hard pavements...

If you only had your old paintbox, you could make a sketch of Shell Mex House with the dawn behind it. But you can hardly keep your eyes open.

You're yawning right in the face of the copper who is looking so hard at you.

Oh, take a taxi and go home to bed.

This radical cure for insomnia is recommended only to gentlemen. It turns them into either excellent sleepers or competent night prowlers—two very good methods of passing the time.

We do not think a lady should walk the streets at night. She can solve her problem by reading some suitable book—*not* a mystery story—but one of the great, admired, educational master-pieces, which will soothe her and instruct her, too.

Don't try to tell us you haven't such a book. What's that in your hand now?

Advice to Those About to Marry

It so happens that this whole vexing question of bed manners is still new.

Until we came along, nobody in this country knew there was such a thing.

All our 45 million people (we aren't including, in this round number, a few brave souls who live all alone on lighthouses and so forth) were just blundering along, hanging up their etiquette every night on the same hook with their clothes— or just leaving it draped over the back of a chair.

To give credit where it is due, it was *Vogue* that first brought up the subject. One of its writers, a Mr Harford Powel, or something like that, challenged all the nicely raised, well-dressed, socially prominent ladies to study the subject of bed manners themselves and try and teach it to their husbands.

Our first book, an absolutely simple little manual for these simple men, came out later—in time for St Valentine's Day.

Now we present this second volume—more advanced, of course. It is for people who have fully grasped the elementary principles, which are:

1. Have all the fun in bed you can.
2. Don't have it at the risk of driving your bedfellow crazy.

Since you understand these two rules, we will merely go on to say that there is something even more important in life than etiquette.

It is charm.

You may cram yourself to the eyes with all the rules of all the etiquette teachers. But no matter how elegantly you eat asparagus, or how correctly you dress yourself for an afternoon wedding, or how carefully you refrain from saying 'Pleased to meet you!' you will nevertheless fail to gain some of life's best prizes unless you have some charm, too.

Is everything clear?

Then we'll end this advanced book with a frank statement that it leaves a lot of ground uncovered. It isn't so much for bachelors and spinsters, of all ages, as it is for people who have plunged right into matrimony in the good old English spirit of learning an art just by practising it. These people need help first. So we have reluctantly left out some very snappy advice on the following useful topics:

Bed Manners in the Army and Navy.
Bed Manners in the Aeroplane.
Fun and Frolic in the School Dormitory.
Do You Walk in Your Sleep?
What every Freshman Should Know.
Common Dreams and What We Are Afraid
    They Mean.

However, it will dry your tears to know that we have all these things in preparation, and that you can soon master every detail of night life—merely by sticking to the old-established firm of Hopton & Balliol.

Meanwhile, keep your eye on charm. Charm is the glue that holds marriages together. Charm is your passport to the best houses and the best bedrooms in those houses. You may be as ugly as a toad, you may not know how to eat asparagus, your toes may be sticking out of the ends of your boots—but if you have charm, your wife will rank you with Galahad, Apollo, Andrew Carnegie and Rudolph Valentino.

Every day begins with a couple of people getting out of bed. Every day ends with those people crawling into it again. That is where charm begins and ends. Even if you don't carry it about all day with you, like a handbag or briefcase, you need it—and lots of it—all night.

A man once won enduring fame by being the author of what was considered one of the funniest jokes ever sent to *Punch*. (This was in the days before bed manners had been invented, and while Hopton & Balliol were still little tots who wondered why most married people looked so gloomy.) Here is the so-called joke:

Advice to those about to marry—Don't!

But if you will preserve the twin principles of being both mannerly and charming in bed, you can go forth on your matrimonial career without fear. You hold the key in your hands. You know the rules. Live up to them. Don't lie down on your bed manners when you lie down on your bed. Then we can give you, if you are still a spinster of seventeen or perhaps a marriageable young man of eighteen or so, a sterling piece of parting advice. It is:

Advice to those about to marry—DO!

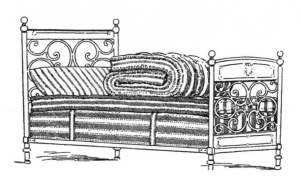